out of the dark

out of the dark

dorothy kavita kumar

This book is a work of fiction. Any references to historical events, real people, or real places are used fictitiously. Other names, characters, places, and events are products of the author's imagination, and any resemblance to actual events or places or persons, living or dead, is entirely coincidental.

Copyright © 2024 by Dorothy Kavita Kumar.

Illustrations and design by Dorothy Kavita Kumar.

All rights reserved. No part of this book may be used or reproduced in any manner whatsoever without written permission.

ISBN: 978-1-7381561-0-8

for kramer

*thank you
for taking my hand
and walking with me
out of the dark
and into the light*

*this is a celebration
of your light*

*i will always be
forever grateful*

eternally yours

there is no darkness
without light
it is the darkness
that is driven out
by the light
and that light my friend
is you

out of the dark

contents

fire	1
rise	25
fly	53
soar	101
light	125

fire

i let the flames wash over me
the transformation has begun
i watch the embers fade away
as the radiance of my reincarnate
gives off the most luminous light

there is still light to give

out of the dark

i have been burned
many times before
but i chose to rise
from my dark ashes
and into the bright flames
lighting up my way

if i can do it so can you

this heavy head
hangs on a tired soul
that has seen the dark
for far too long
but these achy feet
can't help dancing
towards the sun

sundance

out of the dark

lying here
with a clouded head
and heavy lids
the emptiness is real
it has found a home
within my soul
but my divine light
shines bold and strong
it will not let the emptiness
stay here for long

i'm a survivor

place one foot
in front of the other
and you will be just fine
it's not about the number
of steps you take
what matters most
is that you tried

step by step

out of the dark

there are so many ways
in which we give our power away
when we let fear
sit in our hearts and minds
we have given our power
to the greatest thief in the night

fear no more

racing hearts run from fear
afraid of the unknown
which will always
remain unclear
but if fear keeps us away
we may never witness
the endless beauty
that waits for the soul

embrace the unknown

out of the dark

undress your fears
shed away your tears
the time is now
your someday
is here

awakening

dorothy kavita kumar

your day is now

the path of vulnerability
is lined with sweet yellow roses
let the gentle song of the bluebirds
guide you to the end
where you will find
waiting with open arms
courage and all of its friends

being vulnerable makes you beautiful

the thing about courage
is that once you find it
there is no turning back

to infinity

out of the dark

you are more courageous
than you will ever know

leave your fears behind

these shackles
i removed
it was easy to do
once i realized
they are dust
and i am too

freedom

out of the dark

you are the artist
life is your canvas

dream in colour

i often doubt myself
until i remember
that no one else
has the blueprint either

the blueprint

out of the dark

when you believe in yourself
the rest doesn't matter

there will always be doubts

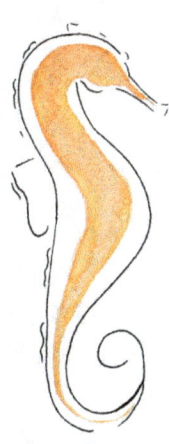

dorothy kavita kumar

stop looking for a hero
start looking in the mirror

there's your hero

out of the dark

there is a strength in me
i did not know
that strength my friend
is in you too

you have the power within

sometimes we think we've come so far
when we've barely walked a mile
sometimes we need to go back to the start
to see how much farther
we still need to run

it takes work

out of the dark

if you want to learn how to fly
you must first learn how to fall

baby steps

you will fall
you will break
you will bleed

you will think this is the end
but it is here that life will meet you
to reveal your resiliency that lies within and

you will find strength
you will find courage
you will start again

never say never

out of the dark

you keep kicking me down
but just like the mountains
i rise from the ground

into the sky

rise

she rose from her ashes
stretched her blackened wings
her talons on the mark
her eyes set on the sun
miles and miles above
but still within reach
she was ready
it was time
to blaze her trail
and leave the rest behind

rise

out of the dark

when i learned
how to love
all of me
this is the love
that set me free

set yourself free

harmony
is the sound you hear
when you learn to love
even the darkest
parts of you

illumination

out of the dark

it was dark within the walls
i had created in my head
the pressure was relentless
the heat was unforgiving
cracks in the walls
slowly started to appear
light began to trickle its way in
and i was finally able to see
the beautiful diamond that was me

shine bright like a diamond

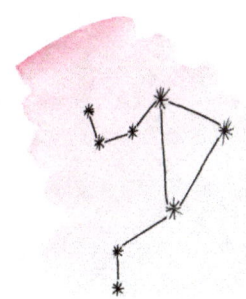

the moon
is glorious
in all its phases
just like you

lunar love

i didn't know myself
until i was reminded of myself
by looking into your brown eyes

i had lost myself
until i was reminded of myself
by looking into your brown eyes

i had missed myself
until i was reminded of myself
by looking into your brown eyes

oh, how good it feels
to see you again
old friend

reflection

i am the ocean
you are the rain
pour your sorrows
into my waves
i'll drown them all away

when i look in the mirror

out of the dark

in a world
where you can choose anything
first choose yourself

self-love is not selfish

dorothy kavita kumar

you are deeper
than the ocean
you gave them
all the reasons
but they couldn't handle
your waves

big waves need big love

learning to love myself
has taken a hold of me
it is a feeling
like no other
one that will stay with me
forever

because i'm happy

they usually realize
when the sun has already set
it's too late now my friend
that's the way this story ends

goodbyes and sunsets

out of the dark

i think of you
like a gentle summer breeze
you cool my skin
and tickle my feet

when i think of me

make me live
i'll show you the stars
make me laugh
i'll take you to the moon
make me love
i'll give you the sun

conversations with myself

out of the dark

love starts
and ends
with you

eternity

kings and queens
come through you
empires stand tall
on your shoulders
that have seen it all

lands that were barren
were resurrected by you
the promise of life
always in your hands

there will never be another
women come together
this world was created by you

giver

out of the dark

you are the most
beautiful soul
i have ever been
blessed to know

self-talk

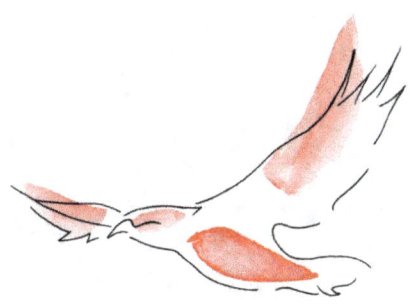

you were created by the hand
and given to the land
to bear the seeds
and labour the fruit
for those who would come
for all of eternity

your power is immeasurable
it lies in the ether
for you are a child
of the sun, the moon and the stars
a gift that is ethereal
may you shine on forever

say her name

your aura is unmatched
you have no rivals
you are beautiful
because you hold
the universe inside you

one in a million

boundless love
is all around you
offering itself each day
all the while showing you
how to give in its wake
this is the love
that makes the willows weep
their crying song carries
on the gentle breeze

weeping willows

out of the dark

we look different
but we smile the same
we talk different
but we hurt the same
we act different
but we love the same

there is only one tribe on earth

one act of kindness
would make you shine bright
and be the light
in someone else's life
for when you gaze up at night
there is nothing better
than a sky full of stars
so let us all be
each other's lights

humankind

out of the dark

happiness is not
something you find
it is planted in your heart
long before you arrive

water your seeds

plant the seeds
to grow your love
tend and nurture
your buds with care
you are the only one who knows
how to make yourself bloom

cultivate self-love

out of the dark

we are all just flowers
reaching for the sun

heliotropic humans

be the sun
rise even when
you feel like setting

solar power

out of the dark

fiercely burning within
flames set my heart ablaze
the wildfire spreads
the glow from the embers
the whisper on the wind
i hear it calling me
the time has come
to go back home

father sun

fly

i have been caged
but never forgot how to fly
now i must soar
with wings that take me
higher than the sky
loudly singing my sweet song
as my shadow graces the fiery sun
burned to the core
i will be no more

free bird

out of the dark

when you choose
to grow through your pain
you give yourself the chance
to meet someone new
the next best version of you

emerge from your chrysalis

we are never truly ready
for what may come our way
when we embrace all the changes
we give ourselves the chance
to experience the abundance
that life has always been offering

the fruit of life

out of the dark

you are the rise
and the fall

duality

i let the darkness wash over me
i usher in the coming of the night
reflections have led me
to a path that has risen
at the soul of me
rebirth has delivered
new power and freedom
for now i know the darkest days
lie just before the brightest dawn
as my fingers slowly reach out
to graze the horizon light

i am not afraid of the dark

out of the dark

some days
the fog remains settled
it is hard to see
two steps in front of me
leaden feet trip me up
nothing seems as it should be

look for the light

dorothy kavita kumar

i end up where i start
the place i run from
always remains in my heart

you can run but you can't hide

still waters run deep
deeper than the eyes can see
but if we wade
far enough into the sea
we can uncover
the darkness that is our deep

the deep end

be the ocean
never be afraid
to explore your dark
and stormy waters

challenge the deep

out of the dark

caught in the eye of the storm
where gale force winds
continue to blow me down
dense fog swirls around
causing layers of clouds
inside of my head
i have learned many times
there is only one way out

push through the storm

break through the levees
as many times as you need
let the water flow over you
so you can wash it all away

healing waters

out of the dark

healing brings you to the dark
it asks you to look around
have a seat and stay awhile
and when you're ready
to see yourself again
take it by the hand
and it will lead you
back to the promised land

follow the leader

the chaos within me
used to love the dark
but i started to shine a light
on what was inside of me
now my chaos walks with me
we stroll along hand in hand
in complete harmony

the art of balance

out of the dark

when i started flooding
my shadows with light
a consequence emerged
i no longer walked in the shade

this little light of mine

grow out of your darkness and chaos
slow and steady
into a light so bright
that even the stars
smile at you

shining

out of the dark

unload this burden
from these shoulders
i unknowingly
gave it permission
i am finally ready
to let it go

growth takes time

growth cannot be rushed
beauty needs time to flourish

the journey is worth it

out of the dark

i let the water fill my ears
the only sound i hear
is the beating of my heart
my body drinks itself up
because i am water
i show you how to swim

flow

what is meant for you
will stay with you
what is meant for you
is yours to face alone

face off

out of the dark

the lies we tell ourselves
the webs we weave
the stories we make up
only to find out
they were all
make believe

sixth sense

to know yourself
is to know that you don't
you are the essence
of the universe
there are no other options
change you must

the constant is change

out of the dark

the image of me
that you have been showing me
for what seems like eternity
is not the image i have of me
the image that i see
is the best version of me

you know yourself best

disjointed
disconnected
many moons removed
from the person i thought
i was supposed to be

new moon

self-imposed
limits on my mind
i shackled my growth
to these cemented vines
i knew i had to start the climb

all the way up

blossom through the bars
of your mind
take time to get lost
within the flowers
of your soul

bed of roses

out of the dark

this is not a man's world
this is not a woman's world
this is a gift we have taken for granted

instead of always taking from her
let us not sever the umbilical cord
that leads to our air

let us instead take the time
to help her flourish and protect her
from our destructive ways

because everyone has
only one mother

without her we do not survive

in a world
with eight billion people
how do we have the ability
to feel so alone
what have we done
to ourselves

echo

out of the dark

we are all trying to connect
in complicated ways
when all we need to do
is the simplest of things

lost in translation

dorothy kavita kumar

misunderstandings
can lead to seas of clarity
but only if you're willing to swim

when you put the work in

out of the dark

words are the tool we use
to express the emotions
that we feel

choose wisely

share with me your pains
show me your sorrows
it's time for us
to turn them into gold

the magic of alchemy

out of the dark

we ebb and flow
like the waves of the sea
one minute we are up
and the next minute
we are crashing down

you are not your emotions

let it roil
let it rumble
emotions must be felt
so they can gently tumble

let the waters settle

i ride the emotions
through my heart
and out of my body
until my mind is free

feeling myself

i am the king
of my thoughts
and the queen
of my feelings

you are the dynasty

out of the dark

once undone
you are now becoming
the very energy
that created the land
that rests beneath your feet

you always had the power

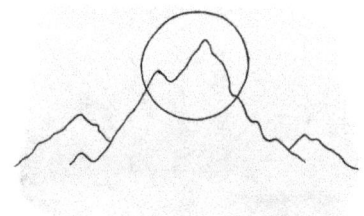

when you are willing to release
all that holds you down
you create space within
to welcome the light
of the stars

star catcher

out of the dark

the only person
that can save you
from yourself
is you

my savior

remind yourself
of why you started
it's simple to forget
the line is easily muddled
always remember to reset

don't lose yourself

out of the dark

when you find your truth
and it sets you free
stay true to it
so that you never cease to be

unlocked

good things don't come
to those who wait
good things come
to those who learn to let go

move forward

out of the dark

your dreams
can be your reality
we are all born
with wings

endless

dorothy kavita kumar

patience brings
pretty rains
sweet rays
and the chance to full bloom

worth the wait

out of the dark

i will dig until i hit the root
and unearth all the beauty that is me
i will water the light and dark seeds
that make up all the parts of me
this is how you discover
the root of the matter

rooted

to love another
you must first learn
to love yourself and

to love yourself
you must first learn
to see yourself and

to see yourself
you must first learn
to accept all that you are

because you deserve it

out of the dark

the longest journeys
have a way
of bringing you
back home

to yourself

soar

nothing feels better
than where you are

self-affirmation

out of the dark

there is nothing wrong
with being alone
we arrive alone
we leave alone

take the time
to be alone
to meet yourself
again and again

surprise yourself
by how much you learn
your knowledge
is your power

the more you know

continue to storm
until you find
the peace of blue

blue skies are waiting

out of the dark

rise over the past
those struggles
are behind you
there are no more troubles
coming to find you

blissful ascension

let it flow
then let it go

ride the wave

out of the dark

we spend so much time
in our minds
that we often forget
how to live

the important part

when i learned
how to be still
i was able to see
with all my eyes
as life began
to unfold itself
through me

third eye

out of the dark

it is in the silence
that the greatest words
are spoken

tune in

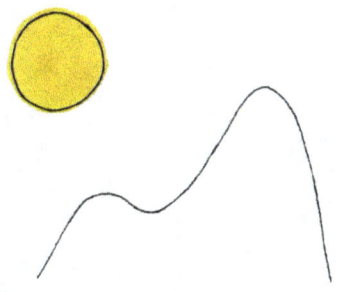

disconnected
time to rejoice
the only thing i hear
is white noise

the sound of my voice

out of the dark

i relish the quiet
it brings with it
the peace that is existence
and it rings loudly
in my ears

hustle and bustle

searching beyond the meadows
and over the hills
seeking around the bends
and under the cliffs
what we search
and what we seek
has always been resting
at our feet

the root of you

out of the dark

laughter
is the heart
speaking

talk to me

turn your madness into music
let the beat move your passion
to the rhythm of the currents
feel the flow of the energy
that is all around you
and pulses through
every part of you

feel the beat

out of the dark

find joy in what you choose
let it seep into your mind
let it flow through your soul
find joy in what chooses you

the universe has other plans

when you feel yourself
slipping away
bring yourself back

lift your head
to the sky above
inhale the air
let it fill your lungs

touch your hands
to the soil below
let the dirt sift
through your fingers

and then remember
what grounds you
to the earth

back to basics

out of the dark

we must return
to our roots
with no fear
they give us strength
and a foundation
to stand tall

bones

i give my love
to nourish my home
so that it continues
to flourish and grow
the cool breeze i feel
from the lush paradise within
balances every part of me
when i'm not feeling like me

it took me time to create a home within

out of the dark

my home is not here
my home is not there
my home is within

i have built a strong foundation

time is my enemy
time is my friend
without time
i simply do not exist

time to transcend

out of the dark

these thoughts
these words
these feelings
these hearts

everything is temporary

i am the air i breathe
i am the love i seek
there is no more that i need
that is all i will take with me

repeat after me

out of the dark

love does not root in the past
love blooms in the present
with water from the heart
and light from the soul

soar

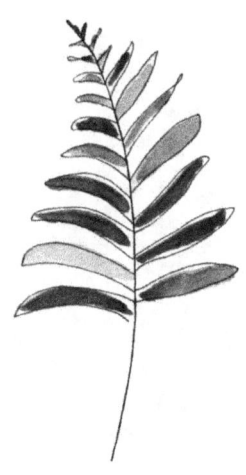

light

your light cannot be dimmed
your greatness cannot be swallowed
as bright as faraway galaxies
you are a beautiful supernova
in disguise

i see you

out of the dark

you are the light
they can no longer contain

shooting star

you are the constant
in your life
you are the constant
just like the light
you are the constant
if you treat yourself right
you are the constant
that will shine bright

starshine

out of the dark

your light
is all the inspiration
you need

look no further

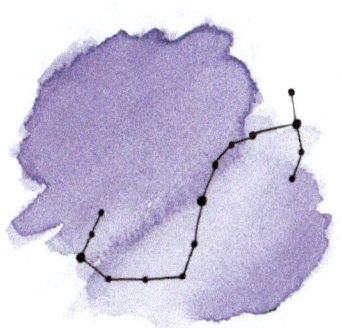

just like the moon
shines brightest
in its darkest hour
i too learned
how to light up
my dark skies

follow the moonlight

every so often
we all shatter
like broken glass
yet our prismatic pieces
oh, they shine so bright
and we have never looked
more beautiful
in all of this light

broken is beautiful

when you learn
to howl at the moon
it becomes easy to spot
the wolves dressed as sheep

by the light of the moon

do not mistake
her kindness for weakness
inside of her is the universal power
that gives rise to humankind
and makes her dark eyes glow
the colour of the sunrise

sun goddess

my mind is free
my heart beats strong
my feet glide along the earth
as i roam where the sky is blue
judgements will never cloud me
the wild things are what surround me

stay wild

out of the dark

we are the hard peaks
of the mountains
that rise from the soft bodies
of the oceans

hard yet soft

you are water
soft and giving
with the power to create
massive ripples

turning tides

out of the dark

you are thunder
and a little bit of lighting
mixed in among the gentle rains

strong yet soft

i wear my heart on my sleeve
it's a beautiful reminder
of where my power lies
not in the emotions i face
but in how i overcome
the obstacles they try to create

there is power in being vulnerable

out of the dark

do not mend
your broken wings
you will learn
to soar again

find the strength in falling

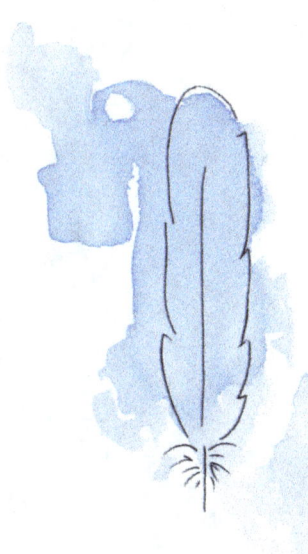

may freedom
give you wings
may your pain transform
to solid ground

smooth landing

out of the dark

tears
are the soul
listening

i'm all ears

dorothy kavita kumar

there is a sweetness
in being your own savior

you are the hero of your story

out of the dark

our eyes tell the stories
that words never can

look beyond

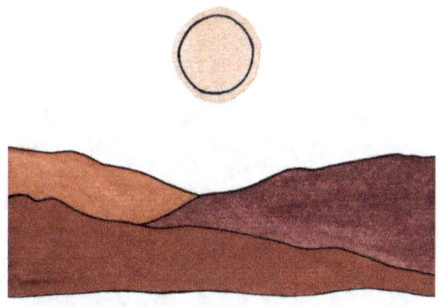

sometimes we must lose it all
to see how much we had
you see we don't need much
we start with nothing
we end with nothing
yet we have always had it all

lose yourself

out of the dark

you will get back there one day
where the sunshine lifts you off your feet
and the universe kisses your cheek

better days are coming

born in a place of light
and unknowingly forming
since you arrived in this world
they will lead you back to the light
if you choose to follow the path
that leads to the yellow brick road

follow your dreams

out of the dark

my existence
is predetermined
i journey through life
in search of its light
hopeful that i might
shine it for all to see

this is my destiny

dorothy kavita kumar

we are creatures of creation
creation is our very existence
take time to create an existence
that lasts beyond your lifetime

the big bang theory

at the root of you
is where happiness blooms
stemming its way
to the heart of you
where kindness nourishes
soft petals that unfold
around the very crown of you
where compassion cultivates
every part of your soul

triple threat

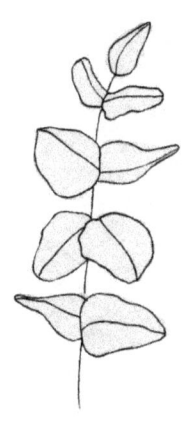

searching and seeking beyond
never finding
releasing and falling within
finally awakening

lost and found

out of the dark

scattered all around
within plain sight
look for the dots
that will lead you
to your soul

connect the dots

on the days where you feel
like giving up the most
don't listen to your mind
learn to feed your soul instead

soul food

out of the dark

once you learn
how to shed the layers
your mind becomes light
like the soul under your skin

time to glow up

dorothy kavita kumar

i let my mind open
like the buds of the earth that grow
i let my heart open
like the layers of air that i breathe
i let my hands open
like the sky full of stars at night
i am now ready to receive

conversations with the universe

out of the dark

listen to the home
that lives inside
your house

trust your intuition

dorothy kavita kumar

pure intentions
no expectations
make for a happy soul

free your mind

out of the dark

you can't hurt
what you can't see
my spirit
will always be free

from here

beauty
is soul deep

out of this world

out of the dark

within you is a light
that glows as bright as the dawn
look inside yourself
and you will find
that your soul is made of gold

twenty-four carat gold

i found the sun
in my soul
it was a glorious day

golden hour

out of the dark

i lost my heart
but i found my soul

this is heaven

be the light
because you are the light

guiding light

with love and light
from me to you

poems, illustrations and cover art by:

dorothy kavita kumar

dorothy kavita kumar is an artist and writer. *out of the dark* is her first poetry collection which she wrote, illustrated and self-published. kavita's work touches on fear, love, healing, presence and spirituality. she lives in british columbia, canada. you can find her online at @dorothykavitakumar.

www.ingramcontent.com/pod-product-compliance
Lightning Source LLC
LaVergne TN
LVHW021948060526
838200LV00043B/1953